The Gettysburg Undress

poems by
Rick Lupert

Gettysburg, PA Washington, D.C.
Mount Vernon Richmond, VA Fred-
ericksburg, VA Baltimore, MD

The Gettysburg Undress

Rothco Press

Cover Image ~ Rick Lupert
Design and Layout ~ Rick Lupert
Author Photo ~ Addie Lupert

Part III of "Walk to Brunch" originally appeared in *Moongarlic E-Zine* Issue 1, November 2013 (www.moongarlic.org)

First Edition ~ May , 2014

ISBN-10: 1941519091
ISBN-13: 978-1-941519-09-7

Published by Rothco Press.
www.rothcopress.com

Visit the author online at
www.PoetrySuperHighway.com

Of what use is an experience if it goes unrecorded?

- from Our House Episode 3 by Nathaniel Mellors

A poem should exist merely for the poem's sake.

- Edgar Allan Poe

He can compress the most words into the smallest ideas better than any man I ever met.

- Abraham Lincoln

Thank you Addie, Brendan, Elizabeth, Audrey and Steve Katz, Jumping Jon, Hal Sirowitz, Suzanne Lummis, Mariano Zaro, Abraham Lincoln and George Washington (Love you guys!!!), Edgar Alan Poe, The Rothco Press crew for making me feel like a million bucks, and the fine people at Pasture Restaurant in Richmond, Virginia who home-make candy bars every day.

*To Addie who lovingly allows me to write about her
while we're attempting to be on vacation.*

on

the

plane

Early Morning Flight

I'd like
to begin
with a nap.

My eyes
have no business
being open.

Even the
o'clock family are
still in their beds.

On the plane
a boy is touching
my arm.

I
know this
boy.

Mistake

We take our son's bear on the plane.
I operate it like a puppet, thinking it
was just washed before the flight

so this is the one time of year it's not
coated with four year old boy slobber
and I can touch it.

I didn't wash the bear Addie tells me,
and the rest of the trip is cancelled
so I can have myself sanitized.

Regarding *'having myself sanitized'*

What I mean was I wanted to get the
boy bear slobber off of me and not
that I'm an overall unclean person,
in case that wasn't clear.

Haiku

I overhear my
wife tell our four year old we're
all out of eyebrows

(This may involve a sticker book)

Oh, the Things That Exist

The SkyMall catalog
has an item called
The Pants Saver.

It is far too late
for my pants.

Paraphrasing the Traveler's Prayer

May it be your will that we arrive
safely at our destination.
Our luggage too.

I'm not sure
I believe in God but
maybe someone on the Internet

will hear and get a
Kickstarter going in case it
falls out of the plane.

My Fifteen Minutes Begins Now

I sneeze super-loud while walking back
to my seat from the bathroom. It's so
loud a large number of passengers
turn to see what had just happened.
At first I'm embarrassed to be the spectacle.
But then I realize all they want is more.
It's finally happening for me I think as I
pray to God (or the internet) for my
allergies to come back.

Jewish Law

Addie shows me the Torah app on her iPad.
Since there's holy text on it, I suggest she's
going to have to bury it.

the

lehigh

valley

Defensive Driving

I've seen people in this
part of the world who

do this thing where
they take off their seat-belts when

they are within a couple blocks of
their destination.

I guess the laws of physics
make that the safe zone.

On the Way to Easton

We pass by the Christian training center.
We pass by the Rock restaurant.
We pass by the Charter School for the Arts.
We pass by Bottom Dollar Food.
We pass by the Candy Factory.
We pass by Walters Foreign Car Service.
We pass by a billboard that says something.
We pass by the Dairy Queen.
We pass by Vic's Bagels.
We stop at a stop light.
We continue when it turns green.
There is the Family Medical Place.
There is the old barn turned condo.
There is the Keystone Pub.
Freedom High School.
The voice of John Lithgow
laughing like he knows
exactly what is happening.
There is something interesting
to say about all of this.

Specialization

At the Just Born Candy Factory
there is a special area just to receive
marshmallow deliveries.
I'm going to stencil "marshmallow receiving"
on my front door and see what happens.

Curiosity

I wonder if it's okay to remove my pants
after passing the sign that says
Welcome to Butztown.
Or am I just pronouncing it wrong?

Saving Time

I don't stop at the sign that says
Free Wood because I figure I've
got that covered.

Technology Dictates the Future

The GPS tells us to
prepare to exit the highway.
I make my preparations.
I want to be ready for this.

At the Crayola Factory

I
At the Crayola Factory
everybody gets a free crayon
which is to be expected.

II
You'd have to really like crayons
to get the annual pass.

No, I stand corrected.
The woman at the sales
desk just told me if you hated crayons

with every fiber in your being, they would
still sell you an annual pass.

III
There is so much to learn
about crayons here.
But I learned very little
because I didn't apply myself.

IV
Everything about this experience
is leading up to seeing the largest
crayon in the world.

V
They have a cafe.
I'll give you sixty-four guesses
what they serve.

VI
There is a whole exhibit on markers.
They're really branching out.

VII
Our four year old enters the multi-room
multi-floor playground structure. I'm pretty
sure we'll never see him again.

VIII
I completely misunderstood
what I was supposed to do in
the *Doodle in the Dark* area and
am quickly asked to leave.

IX
In one area you stand in front of
an animated crayon who mimics
whatever motions you make.
After a short time it becomes clear
it is just mocking you.

X
There is no explanation as to why
there are sharpeners in the bathrooms.

XI
We have twelve nights left on this trip.
But after seeing the largest crayon in the world
in Easton, Pennsylvania, as far as I'm concerned
this vacation is over.

XII
We see the marketing department at work
when we come across the *Extreme Coloring* exhibit.

XIII
I wonder if there was confusion during the days
of the old radio scandals and they tried to pay radio DJs
in crayons to play their songs.

XIV
Like most amusement parks there is a special area to
detain people who are misbehaving. Here they call it
Crayon Jail. Ironically it's the only place here they don't
segregate by color.

XV
They sell *Naked Juice* at the cafe.
This causes much giggling among the four year old set.
And their father.

en

route

to

gettysburg

Affirmative Action

The GPS seems to have a speech impediment.
I'm glad they didn't discriminate when they hired her.

Truth in Advertising

Easton, Pennsylvania has a bar called *Drinky's*.
When I get home I'm going to open a restaurant
called *Eatie's* and maybe a nail salon called *Fingie's*.

In One Store

I see American themed underwear
with red white and blue firecrackers on it.
Oh yes, tomorrow, there will be an explosion.

At Breakfast in Whitehall

The man at the next table
tells his son he won't get
a birthday gift if he doesn't behave.
This is a promise he can't possibly keep.
Later he sends back a plate of
hash-browns because they "came too late".
This is something he has power over.
I overhear a police radio in his pocket.
We are dining with the law that
never gets turned off.

En Route to Gettysburg

Towards the end of The Romantic's song
What I Like About You, where they are singing *hey* over and over,
we pass by a big sign on the side of a barn that says "Hay".
I can't think of a moment more perfect than this.

The song is immediately followed by Pearl Jam, *Alive*
as if Eddie Vedder himself saw the sign too.
Perfect.

As I dictated the last poem to my wife

so I wouldn't drive off the road
destroy part of rural Pennsylvania

and kill everyone I love,
when I got to the line about

never experiencing a more perfect moment
she interjected, *how about our wedding day*

Can't I just write one poem by myself on this trip,
I respond.

As I dictated the last poem to my wife

while she was typing it
her eyebrows were raised
with a certain spousal judgment.

We Drive by the Huddlesville Hotel

I can't imagine
that's good for anyone's back.

Or perhaps this is how
teams of football players sleep.

I'm Very Tired and Realize I've Never Mentioned Eye Boogers in a Poem

Don't you think it's about time?
(Addie responds with her best *midget on a coffee break* voice,
no.)

We Pass by Funcks Family Restaurant

I wonder if they added the "n" at Ellis island.
I love you America.

the
gettysburg
undress

The Gettysburg Undress

It is so hot
in Gettysburg, Pennsylvania
all we want to do is deliver
the Gettysburg Undress.

Out of Time

A man dressed in Civil War era clothing
holds up a camcorder. The anachronism
is hurting me.

Where Did He Say What He Said?

There is no marker at the exact spot
where Lincoln gave his address.
One of the park rangers will tell you
where it is. The other will just tell you
in a disappointed fashion, if you don't
want to go on the tour *that's the trick*.
You'd think, one of the most famous speeches
In history, they'd put up a sign or something.

Animal Hospitality

They put an acorn on each of the graves
in the soldiers cemetery. This encourages
squirrels to visit at night. So the soldiers
won't be lonely.

Believe it or Not Capitalism Has Come to Gettysburg

Here you can stop into the *Battlefield Mini Market* and
buy a bottle of *Gettysburg Label* root beer.
Or head across the street to the restaurant where
they serve *Battlefield Fries.* Imagine the patriotism
of eating the hand cut deep fried potatoes
of the Union Army, topped with *Lincoln's Beard*
ketchup. We drive to Washington D.C.
where it all began.

You Can Buy a Mustache Lollipop in the Fudge Shack in Gettysburg

I think that's a thing invented by men who wanted
other people to touch their lips with theirs.

One House on Baltimore Pike in Gettysburg proudly displays a Confederate Flag

News travels slow in certain parts of the world.

At Gettysburg Haiku

I
We see thousands of
unmarked graves. Tell me what is
civil about war?

II
And you could answer
What is civil about men
owning other men?

we drive in
the rental car to
washington in the
district of columbia

Getting Into It

We enter the state of Maryland.
Cross the Mason-Dixon line.

I pull out my pocket sweet tea
and press the button that enacts my southern drawl.

I feel a case of the vapors coming on.
And the cotton is high.

We Pass By a Sign Advertising a Lions Club Barbecue

I don't know if this is
a group of humans who serve lion,

or a club of lions
who serve whatever the hell they want.

In either case, our vegetarianism
prevents us from finding out.

Children, Don't Read This

I misread a sign that says *Gusty Winds Area*
as *Guilty Winds Area* and think
My God, who did they blow now?

I Admit It

My wife tells me she is challenging her brain
with the puzzles on her iPad. I ask her

*Don't you think being married to me
challenges your brain enough?*

She does not answer,
which is answer enough.

Ramifications

We see flashing lights on a sign which reads
If lights are flashing you are going too fast.
I flash it right back which causes a whole
other set of lights to go off

Let This Be Real

I see what looks like a naked person
in their back yard by the pool.
I think they're naked.
I want it to be true.
I just need this one thing.

Geography with Rick Lupert

Maryland looks like it was sliced off Pennsylvania
so it would have a smooth bottom.
Either that or Pennsylvania is Maryland's lobotomy.

Boobversation

I think I see my wife cleaning her iPad with her boob.
She assures me that did not happen.
But at least I got her to say
Boob did not touch iPad.
My job here is done.

I Guess This is How It Is Now

My wife asks

Would it be alright if you heard
some animal sounds now?

I'm not sure if she's referring to
a game on her iPad or

if that's just the direction
she's going in from this point on.

we arrive in
washington d.c.
and do things which
are documented on
the following pages

New Glory

Addie wants to gather up all the people in D.C.
wearing elements of the American flag on their clothing
and make them stand in various positions so Old Glory
will be revealed. I think this is the best idea since
Betsy Ross first came up with the idea of flinging
vegetarian chicken fingers off the Washington Monument.

There are Pictures of Corn on the Cob Lining the Walls of the Bathroom at Founding Farmers Restaurant.

It's not helping.

Making Fun of the Lesser Mollusks

I
We aren't sure what scallops are
so Addie looks it up on Wikipedia.
She starts to read the entry
Scallops do not have brains, therefore
and I interrupt, *They're idiots.*
What's on your mind scallop, I might ask.
Nothing, it would imply.

II
Upon learning that scallops have no brains
I decide to never ask one for directions.

The Fourth of July

I am sitting on the lawn beneath the Washington Monument
pulling leaves of American Grass out of the ground.

I'd like to think it was Benjamin Franklin who invented photosynthesis,
But despite the freedoms afforded me after the efforts of The General,

this is not the case. No one will tell you the best place to see the fireworks
or they will all tell you something different.

We trust our choice was good by the thousands of
human evidences who surround us.

Either that or we are all wrong. I'm going to trust my gut on this,
and come ten after nine the sky will explode in front of our very eyes.

A Family Abandons Their Blanket

I
We assume they will come back but
we consider taking it over in the
American spirit of *Blanketfest Destiny.*

II
That's right spellcheck, *Blanketfest.*
You're going to have to deal with it.

Disappointing News

One D.C. newspaper has the headline "Ecuador Debunked." Man, I thought that place was real.

At The Spy Museum

I
We are preparing to go to the Spy Museum.
I eye Addie suspiciously over my tea mug.
She points out she is wearing all black so
she can not be seen. I mention that only
works at night. And if you aren't Caucasian.
We sip more tea, and hope that it's not poisoned.

II
Addie, in her black dress, tries to blend in with
the black lampposts on 8th street. I think it works.
No KGB agents notice her.

III
When we enter the Spy Museum
The agent at the door tells us
No flash photography.
Of course not my friend,
I respond with a wink and
a nod to the hidden camera
in my eyebrow.

IV
Every five minutes
I give Addie a subtle nod, confirming
something or other.

V
I am suspicious of everyone.

VI
The brochure says
A spy must live a life of lies.
So when the man takes our tickets
I tell him *I'm eleven feet tall.*
This is the life I've chosen.

VII
I tell Addie "it's awfully humid outside
Don't you think?" Which I mean as spy
code for something important.

VIII
There is a cloak room here.
With this much detail you think they would
have called it the *Cloak and Dagger* room.

IX
I head into the bathroom where
I deport some counter agents.
(Kagel G.B.)

X
When the Japanese combined two of
the world's most awesome things to create
The Ninja Spy they set a new bar for
espionagical awesomeness.

XI
The name of one carrier spy pigeon
was *Black Check Cock* which
requires no commentary.

XII
At the end we stand near the entrance.
A young girl comes up to us and asks if
we are there for the *Spy Mission.*
You have already failed, I tell her.

XIII
We complete our mission at the Spy Museum.
Now I need you to set this book on fire.
DENY EVERYTHING!!!!

XIV
And then I never see Addie again
after I begin to cross a street and
she is stuck looking at a baby in an Ergo.

At the National Gallery of Art

I
Some of the early Monets don't look
like Monets at all which shows you
what the hell I know.

(Nothing.)

II
The Peppermint Bottle
Paul Cezanne, 1893/1895

I am relieved that Cezanne's painting
The Peppermint Bottle
Is not called *The Peppermint Battle.*

III
Parau ne te Varua ino
Paul Gaughin, 1892

Addie is disappointed when in front of
Gaughin's "Words of the Devil" featuring
two naked ladies, one with a shocked
look on her face. All I could think of
to say was *somebody must have
said something.*

IV
Portrait of a Boy
Chaim Soutine, 1928

You look a little cocky I'd probably tell
the bow legged boy with his arms on his hips
if I could go back in time and speak to the model.

On the other hand if I could go back in time
I'd probably just find myself as a baby and
tell me to buy low and sell high.

V
One Exhibit is Called "Orientalism and The Nude"
I can't wait to get to the "Anglosaxism and
the Revealed Tushy" room.

Jazz at The National Sculpture Garden

I
The security guard
at *Jazz in the Sculpture Garden*
dances, which makes me feel
more secure.

II
I'm listening to *The Girl From Ipanema.*
Not just the song, but the girl singing it
who is from Ipanema. What are the odds

this double whammy of convergence
would unveil itself to me here in the

National Gallery Sculpture Garden
which is either open until seven PM

or eight thirty.
The sign isn't very clear.

III
They point the band away from
the majority of the people
which is how it works here
in Washington, D.C.

IV
The Girl From Ipanema echoes
in the form of whistling in the
Sculpture Garden Cafe bathroom.
This is the power of music.

V
*The obligatory mention of going to the bathroom while traveling
in Rick Lupert's poetry which I believe has already happened in this
collection so you shouldn't be surprised about this and, yes, please
judge me for this.*

It's amazing how
the absence of toilet paper
in a public bathroom can
ruin your whole day.

VI
We are Going to eat at a Place Called *Oyola*.
It's a Mexican restaurant and
apparently not a scandal involving
Jewish Radio Disc Jockeys.

VII
During the jazz band's break
they put on P-Funk - *Flash Light*.
I've never been more okay with
a prerecorded musical selection.

VIII
I don't blame the ladies in front of us
for not sharing their pitcher of sangria
despite my longing looks. This is not
communism, after all.

IX
In D.C. you can walk down the street
with a pitcher of sangria you purchased
at the cafe in the sculpture garden.
It is not legal and you will be arrested.
But you could still do it.

X
An Asian family is blocking my view of the band.
With enough public support and funding
there may one day be a memorial to this
incident too here on the National Mall.

XI
I'm just waiting for someone to
spill a pitcher of Sangria on my new
white shirt. *Sangriafest Destiny.*

XII
There is a civil war happening
between my nose and the smell
coming from the woman sitting
up-wind from me.

XIII
The band is flute heavy. They're good but
I'd rather them be something else heavy.

XIV
I see a man with three teeth nearby.
Though to be honest that's a rough estimate.
I didn't get in there and count.

XV
At the end of one song a *jazz-rave*
breaks out between the security guard
and a woman walking by.

XVI
The Joan Miro sculpture
Gothic Personage, Bird-Flash
looks like a vagina.

Suitably for this public area
is a sign next to it which reads
Do not enter.

It is a Washington D.C. Midnight

Motor vehicle sounds pay no mind
to our triple paned hotel windows.

There is disconcernment the *blackout curtains*
do not completely black us out.

Our legs and stomachs have
done the work of a bucket of men today.

Addie pulls the pillow away, not knowing my
head was sharing it with hers.

It is okay. The bed offers a
Bill of Rights of pillows.

One for every appendage.
One for every monument.

Our second night in this city has come
and is going.

Eumania

Today we went to a museum.
Tomorrow a *Newseum*.
We will go to anything
with *eum* in it.

There is a Clamshell Shower in Our Hotel Room

And by this I mean
take a clam shell.
Put it on its side.
(Assume the clam
is not still in there)
Then make it
as tall as the ceiling.
Now walk in the entrance
where the clam would come out.
Walk around the spiral until
you reach the controls.
Operate the controls.
Now continue in the spiral
to where water is coming
out of the ceiling.
You are the clam
taking a shower
inside your shell.
Now that I think about it
I don't know why
they call it clam shell
since it's really more like
a snail or hermit crab.
I guess they don't
like to talk about crabs when
referring to your shower.

P.S. There is no shower curtain or door
P.P.S. You don't need one.
P.P.P.S. There is only one way out.

I Have a Dream (Of Peeing)

The Men's bathroom at *Busboys and Poets*
had picture of Martin Luther King, Jr. on the door
which made me feel like I was making a difference
when I went in there.

After Seeing a Sign Advertising the *Koshland* Science Museum

I wonder if they focus
on Jewish sciences such as
potato pancakeology
and oynetics.

At The Newseum

I
I'm at the Newseum
There should be a Jewseum.

II
The *express elevator* to the sixth floor is slow.
They should call it the *nonstop yet kind of slow elevator.*

III
In the Newseum giftshop
my wife picks up a Teddy Bear
iPad holder and says
That would be helpful in bed.
I've never been more humiliated.

IV
I misread a sign at the beginning of the
interactive newsroom exhibit that says

*Sitting in the hot sea*t as
Shitting in the hot seat.

That's the one of things you
don't want to broadcast.

V
The special effects in the Newseum's 4D film
move your chair, blow wind, and run something
against your legs to make you experience the fate
Nellie Bly did when she pretended to be insane.
For the next several hours Addie brushes her fingers
against me, keeping the simulation going beyond
its natural boundaries.

VI
After I pose in a position that I find hilarious
next to a statue, as if I'm part of the scene,
it occurs to me I would make a great coffee table book.

VII
The Newseum bathroom walls
have tiles with funny news blooper headlines
that make bathroom walls in all other museums
seem sad and uncommunicative.

At The National Portrait Gallery

I
Nathan Pierce,
our nations fourteenth president
had a shock of dark hair
drooped over the side of his face
that undoubtedly endeared him
to the goths of his day. And also
the Cosmo Kramers.

II
There is no portrait of Obama
in the National Portrait Gallery's
exhibit of American Presidents.
News travels slow in certain
parts of the world.

III
We see a slow moving video
traveling along what must be legs.

I ask Addie if she thinks
its going to end in crotch or feet

as we can't tell what direction
it's going in.

Addie says crotch because
why would you want to climax with feet.

I agree and tell her *you're right*

the crotch always climaxes.

She feels like she set herself up for that
but then it turns out we were both wrong

as it kept going after crotch
and culminated with head.

I guess we forgot for a moment
we were in the National Portrait Gallery.

IV
I asked a staff member why there was no Obama portrait
In the American Presidents exhibit and their eyes got wide
and they exclaimed *Oh, shit!* and ran off in the direction
of the museum offices.

V
TV Chair
Nam June Paik, 1968

In the modern art video gallery
one piece is a chair with a transparent seat
with a TV under it, screen pointing up.
It's about time they developed television
exclusively for the anus.

VI
Untitled (prepared Scroll)
Collage of Asian wall scroll, photograph of
Charlotte Moorman performing, 1969/1974

At one piece Addie says
TV boobed cello player?
to me inquisitively.
You're just going to have to come to D.C.
to interpret this one for yourself.

VII
We only have twenty minutes left
so we skip the big splotches of color paintings room
altogether.

VIII
I pose excruciatingly long for some photos
which serves me right for making Addie
shoot me in all these ridiculous poses.

It's Sheep Month at the Cheese Shop on F Street

Oddly this has nothing to do with the cheese.

Addie says "I feel a lot better since the crack."

I know she's referring
to something about her foot.
But still, she can't blame me for
writing these things down.

Emissaries

for Audrey and Jumping Jon

Friends greet us with
souvenirs of the occasion
and arms wrapped around our bodies
and smiles, and one of them even
jumps up and down, as is his custom.
It is so good to be a friend.

At Co Co. Sala

I
The chocolate covered bacon
is enough to make you want to
leave both vegetarianism
and Judaism.

II
I wonder if you have to leave the restaurant
if you order the *cheese excursion.*

Age Test with Rick Lupert

Do you feel your age?
asks one man. So I
take my hands and touch
different parts of my body,
pause to consider, then answer.
No, about ten years younger
which gives me an idea for a
new kind of *Guess Your Age* booth.

We Pass by Legal Sea Foods

I'm glad the restaurants
in this city of law
are taking it seriously.

We Are Staying in a
Spy Themed Hotel

So when the elevator door opens
(We are inside) I tell Addie to say nothing
in case someone gets inside.

No one gets on and Addie proceeds to
do a thematic dance to the music
playing on the elevator speakers.

This was not part of the plan.

Curious

I wonder, at the restaurant called
Lincoln on Vermont Street,
if they serve real Lincoln meat.

Walk to Brunch

I
Ducks in a park
near the White House.
These are the ducks of liberty.

II
Men sleeping on benches
in a park. This is the cost
of liberty.

III
I'm wearing a shirt that might be purple.
I'm not sure how it's come to this.

Wait To Eat Brunch

I
If you don't have to wait
thirty to forty-five minutes
to be seated for brunch
you are probably not
at the right restaurant.

II
A party of four catches me snapping a photo
of a cute woman outside the restaurant window.
I want to tell them it's my wife before they report me
for public creepiness. But it looks like they're
going to let it slide.

III
A man with pastel green pants
walks into the restaurant.
As if this is any way to behave.

After Brunch Walk to
the Space Museum

I
We're going to the Air and Space Museum.
But our expectations are tempered as we hear
they clutter up the air and space with a lot of exhibit.

II
We pass by the *Editors Building* where
everything I've written so far is erased.
And my brain.

At the Air and Space Museum

I
I head in to the men's room
at the Air and Space Museum
where I experience first hand
the struggle against gravity.

II
I think it's funny
when Addie tells me
to adjust my fly here
in the flight museum.

III
Even the elevator here
is kind of exhilarating.

IV
It occurs to me here
for some reason
that flash photography
is not taking photographs
of flashers.

V
All I've been saying this whole time
I tell Addie, *is that if we had our own*
aircraft carrier, we could live on it and
have enough space for anything we needed.
She claims this is the first she's heard of this.
I think she's been missing the signs.

VI
With all the technology on display
in the space area of the museum
you'd think the upstairs bathrooms
would be operational.

VII
Despite Pluto's downgrade to
Dwarf Planet status, it still has
a good amount of sentimental
display in the *Planets Room.*

VIII
Two brothers from Ohio
perfected heavier than air travel,
so oceans could be crossed
continents could be reached
and the heavy burden of
humans or bombs could be
brought home.

IX
I pass by the *Satellite Systems in Jeopardy*
explanatory text without reading it.
I know I'm going to kick myself later
when one is falling out of the sky
and my knowledge of the situation
could have prevented it.

X
According to a sign I just read
It would only take about an hour to drive to space.
You would, however, need an off road vehicle.

XI
Like the Hebrews of Biblical Egypt
Pluto has been completely stricken
from the record of planets.

XII
Because of the crowds
there is very little space
in the space museum.

XIII
The Cold War ended for a brief moment
in 1975 when U.S. and Russian space craft
kissed on the nose for a few days and
astronauts played chess.

XIV
I just touched a moon rock.
This is the greatest adventure
my finger has ever been on.

This is only one of the great adventures
my finger has been on.

The Scenery Changes

Addie is not feeling well and heads back to the hotel. So now nothing cute is going to happen for the next several pages of this book.

Wrong Entrance

I walk up the giant welcoming entry stairway
of the National Archives Museum. Must be fifty steps!

My legs, vehicles to discover the documents of my nation's past.
Only to discover a security guard at the top pointing to a small door,

down the stairs, at the side of the building.
Ladies and gentlemen, your tax dollars at work!

Oblivion

I've become so comfortable with the grid street system
here in D.C. Numbered streets going north and south
lettered streets east and west. I feel like I'm taking
a great risk, after three days, turning down one of the angled
streets, named after U.S. states, which heads God knows where.

More Power to Her

My phone's battery is running low.
I ask Addie to email me some power
from back at the hotel. She's so cute,
she does it.

Second of Three Poems Written at the National Museum of Crime and Punishment

A sign tells me
More violent crime happens in the west
than anywhere else in the country.
A tear streams down my face...
land that I love.

Here's the Third

I feel like America's least wanted.
when I stand in the set of *America's Most Wanted*
for ten minutes and nothing happens.

This Is Still Happening

I pass by the Spy Museum
on the way back to the hotel.
I say nothing.

Chocolate City

I'm pretty sure I see Doctor Funkenstein
taking a nap on a bench on H Street.
He deserves a rest after all of his efforts
to turn the White House black.

At the Famed 2 Amys Pizza Restaurant in North West D.C.

The pizza here is certified by the Italian government.
I will no longer eat foods that are not certified by

the country from which they come.
Two people recommended this place. I thought the

first one had said *3 Amys,* so when the second
person brought it up I ask if one of the Amys had died,

and they laughed like I was the funniest
person in the world.

Addie Asks What Else is Unique to D.C. In Terms of Dessert.

I suggest chocolate Obama-balls and she is just glad
the waitress was ten seconds too late to hear it.

Work In Progress

I'm working on a project where
I combine the words
Neapolitan and *Politician.*
I'll let you know how
it turns out.

Still at 2 Amys

Because we are
on vacation we
order two pizzas.
This is also
because we
are idiots.

the day we leave
washington's city
and go to his house

The "Yellow Cabs" in DC are Orange

I have a problem with this.

It's Like We're Floating on an Escape Raft In the Middle of The Ocean After Vanquishing the Megalomaniac

When I check out of the spy themed hotel
I tell them *Mission Accomplished*
They give me a *yeah, he gets it* smile.
The mission truly is accomplished.

On the way to Mount Vernon

We pass Fordson Road
which I read as *Foreskin Road*.
The wound never heals.

At Mount Vernon

I
The outside bathroom
was called
The Necessary.

I know
there've been a lot of bathroom
references so far

but that
just seemed
interesting.

II
Washington was sent the key to the Bastille
after it was destroyed. It has been hanging
on the wall here since 1789. We're not
allowed to take pictures inside the mansion
so I will describe it for you:

It's a really big key.

III
The *Meet Lady Washington* room
is closed which is too bad because I wanted to
sit on her lap and tell her what I wanted
for Hanukkah.

IV

Everything you see here shows you a picture of
George Washington, the general, the President
the great man. Then you learn he owned upwards
of three hundred slaves who worked here.
His *Last Will and Testament* freed them upon
his death in 1799. When he was done with them.

V

Whenever Addie points at some object
or tree stump and says "can I sit on this"
disaster will surely follow.

VI

We're waiting for the tour guide at *George Washington's
Gristmill and Distillery* and Addie asks if I want to pretend
to be the guide and get things going. Of course I do so
in my tour guide voice I ask the assembled crowd of
Addie and the tree *who knows what grist is.* No audible
answer comes but I continue *that's right.* Addie interrupts
me to point out one of my shirt buttons is undone and my
fly is halfway down. This ends the tour.

VII

I learned everything there is to know
about George Washington today
except what was in the letters
that Martha burned.

License Plates

It says *Taxation Without Representation*
on Washington, D.C. license plates
which I feel would be better on the
license plates of the Redcoats.

It says *Don't Tread On Me*
on Virginia's license plates
which is why its residents float
from destination to destination
like detached dandelion spores
not one toe ever touches the ground.

TV Has Informed Me

We pass through Quantico, Virginia
which is, I assume, where they store
idle FBI agents who mention it so often
when they are not appearing in
the prime time shows I so fancy.

We Drive Through Spotsylvania

where we see nothing but vampire dogs.

richmond, virginia
city of things
they have there
(not official slogan)

Telephone

Addie looks at the Richmond map
and says *They have a telephone museum of Virginia.*
I turn to the empty seat to my right and say
They have a mellophone museum of virgoonya.
It takes her a second but she gets it.

Good Morning Richmond

Addie
complains about the water on
the bathroom floor.

I tell her
I can't be held responsible
for the things I cause.

I say it
so convincingly, she almost
buys it.

This is Still Still Happening

The restaurant we eat breakfast at
has a "secret burrito."
The mission continues.

At Citizen, Richmond

Everyone is a citizen at *Citizen*.
They know your name when you walk in the door.
They know the food you want to put in your mouth.
You have the right to replace your greens with fruit.
This is our first stop on the *Richmond Liberty Trail*
No better way to begin.

Finials

for Elizabeth Iannaci

I first heard the word *finial* from you, Elizabeth.
Now I stand in front of the largest I've ever seen
from the Virginia Capital, circa 1861.
Larger than all the human heads we hold so dear.
I think of you, across the country, and hope
with the sincerity of a confederate soldier
your curtains remain well appointed
your denied goldfish visible through
the open window.

At the Confederate Gift Shop

I pick up a Civil War themed paddle ball paddle
and ask Addie if we should get this to spank Jude with
when he commits his occasional northern aggression.
She answers a resounding *NO* with the finality of
an Appomattox.

We Tour the White House of the Confederacy

I
Richmond, Virginia, so close to D.C. The presidents
could have met for lunch every day. If only enemies
ate a meal together so many more boys would
never have left their mothers.

II
It would be funny if instead of labeling the bathroom doors
Men and *Women,* they labeled them *Northerners* and *Southerners.*
Clearly the people at the American Civil War Center do not publicly
share my sense of humor.

After Today's Civil War Immersion

The story of the *Emancipation Proclamation*
The African American hotel shuttle driver
ferrying us from location to location
After all that, when the man asks if
I want the black iced tea, my heart bleeds
an *oh, yes* out of my mouth
Addie chooses the peach
and we walk hand in hand
up Main Street Richmond
a beacon of solidarity

I'm Eating an Apple
in Richmond, Virginia

They say an apple a day keeps the doctor away.
Well I haven't seen a doctor since the great
unconsciousness of 2010 and the number
of days since then has far outnumbered
the number of apples.

Secrets

While sipping peach iced tea
Addie visits the *Naked Scientist dot com*
website for reasons
I'm not allowed to tell you.

Anticipation

I can't wait to find out what kind of
goth fuckers work at the Edgar Allan Poe museum.

At the Poe Museum

I
My enthusiastic, sunny day greeting
does not go over well with the darkly demeanored
ticket seller at the Poe museum.

II
I do the math wrong and think, at first,
Poe married his thirteen year old cousin
when he was thirty eight. After a little more reading
I see he was actually only twenty seven
which, Addie and I agree, is much better.

III
Poe was paid for his first collection of short stories
with twenty five copies of the book. There's still hope
for all of us.

IV
Poe was jealous of the Northern writers who
looked down upon the Southern states.
The literary seeds of the Civil War
sowed with his pen.

V
Poe was removed from a New York literary salon
by Anna Charlotte Lynch after "indiscreet" letters to him
from married women were discovered.
Unfortunately for Poe, there was no method to
delete your cache or browser history back then.

VI
Poe's boot books. Poe's boot
hooks. I'm looking at Poe's boot
hooks. It's Poe's boot hooks!

VII
Poe and Baudelaire
believed in the supremacy
of short poems.

VIII
Poe was immortalized on a stamp
which I shall now refer to as a
Poe-stage stamp.

IX
I refer to the little finger puppet
of Poe as *Finger Poe-pet*
for the enjoyment of all.

X
As we leave the Poe museum,
the bookstore worker says "Have a great day"
in a cheerful manner which delegitimizes
the whole experience.

I Leave the Cucumber Man To You

Addie wants to know
if I notice the guy walking
down the street with
a cucumber under
his arm.

I did not
so you will
just have to
read about that
in her book.

Slap-slip

While walking through an area of town
Known as *Shockoe Slip,* I feign slipping
and look at Addie and announce proudly
Shockoe SLIP! At which point she gives me
one of the longest looks I've experienced from her.

Capital City

The empty store fronts
in Richmond outnumber
the full ones.
The North is still winning.

Quote At the Reconciliation Statue

Forgiveness does not change the past.
But it does enlarge the future.

Paul Boese

(Is anyone mad that this entire poem consists only of
a quote by someone else?)

Paved Paradise

We go to the spot of the slave auction house.
Instead of a the slave auction house, we find
they have put up a parking lot.

I'd rather have a place to park
than a place where humans are sold
but a memorial would have been nice.

We Walk on a Bridge Crossing Interstate 95

I point to the left and say
look we could walk all the way to Miami.

at which point Addie stops suddenly
and gives me the holy hell fire of all looks.

She has had enough
of my shenanigans.

Pulling a Nin

I ask Addie if certain things
which I'm not allowed to write about
could be released twenty years
after our deaths. She says *maybe.*

Murder Park

We successfully navigate through
what one *Yelper* refers to as
Murder Park without being murdered
only to almost be killed by
an ambulance which, I feel,
would be very bad luck.

george washington
was a boy once near
fredericksburg,
virginia

We're Coming to Your Town Too

Addie is glad I wrote something
about Spotsylvania earlier
as something needed to be said
about that name.

On the Banks of the Rappahannock River

On the boyhood property of George Washington
an electric guide tells us everything.

The sun burns my neck.
The grass wets my toes.

You can imagine a young boy
throwing a silver dollar sized rock across.

We are excited to do the same.
They don't tell you, though,

you have to bring your own rock.
The strength of a nation

is forged on a rock
thrown across a river.

At the Bourbon Distillery Tour

I

I drag Addie to the bourbon distillery tour.
I have no idea how I got home after that.

II

They offer free souvenir bungs
at the A. Bowman Smith Distillery.
And now I know what a bung is.

III

I wish I could do justice to the smell of the distillery.
Suffice it to say I want to eat the air out of this room.

IV

Everyone gets a free bung
We take ours and for the rest of the trip
look for holes to fill with it.

V

After the five samples
I begin to tell Addie every thought I've ever had.
She describes it as *bourbon crack.*
This is The Matrix.

Walking Fredericksburg

I
In Fredericksburg
they're advertising a
Beard and Mustache
Competition.

I wonder if the beards
and mustaches compete
disembodied from their
face growers.

II
I can't fault the *Griffin Bookstore
and Coffeeshop* for not having any
Brautigan on their shelves.
Not every establishment needs
to cater to my obsession.

III
I see a sign in the bookstore which reads
Please Do Not.
So I don't.

IV
The bookstore a block away
has a Brautigan on the shelf
The first one I read.*
Fredericksburg is saved.

* The Abortion

V

One store is having a
twenty-five percent off sale
on Civil War artifacts.
Now that the war is over
There is less of a call
for these things.

VI

Thank God for
Fredericksburg, Virginia
It's welcome center and
it's mighty public
restrooms.

VII

At the tea shop
in Fredericksburg, Virginia
they sell products made in
Fredericksburg, Ohio.
Nepotism.

VIII

It is close to Bastille Day and
French flags line Caroline Street.
This reminds me of the Bastille key
at Mount Vernon.

What about you?

IX
We assume the possessive of
Fredericksburg is *Fredericksburg's*
It is very hard to say.

Try it.

(Please note we are not insured for
whatever happens to your mouth)

baltimore, maryland
we head to you and
then are in you

While driving to Baltimore

My wife says *sticky balls*
At first I'm embarrassed but then
I realize she's looking at the menu
of an Asian restaurant

P.S. they also offer the *Dirty Vegan*

I Blow Addie a Kiss When We Cross Chopawamsic Creek

It is our custom to kiss
when we cross over water
But I tell you this more so
I can include the name
Chopawamsic in this collection

Several More Observations on the 95

I
Because of the traffic
we may not eat dinner for hours.
So we eat nuts in the car.
Not the sticky ones.

II
Addie notes the city *Dumfries*
is probably not pronounced *dumb fries*.
Though when was the last time
you saw a potato build a rocket to the moon?

III
Addie also notes *Manassas*
is not pronounced *man asses*.
Neither of us are sure whether
or not to be disappointed.
Still we'd love to see the museums there
as would our four year old who
constantly reminds us that
naked is funny.

IV
We pass by *Backlick Stream Valley Park.*
Man if I could lick my own back
I would never have to pay rent again.

One restaurant is closed

with the word *funeral* taped to the door.
We don't know if that's what they normally serve
or if there is a funeral inside instead of the restaurant
or if it is a foreboding sign of what's to come if we ate their food?
We head to the restaurant down the street.

We Ask the Waiter about the *Dirty Vegan* on the Menu

He says he is one
but not the other.

Later all is revealed
when he tells us

he is not a vegetarian.
His quick wit and mine

co-mingle. I tell him
we should take this on the road.

It earns us the
friends and family discount.

We take our tots home
neatly wrapped in a sushi box.

Three Restaurants in Fells Point

One called *Liquid Earth*
to which I will bring a bathing suit.

One called *Ding How* at which
I will do a jig of joy in front of.
Dig now!

And one called *One-Eyed Mike's*
at which I will dine heartily
and tip with tales of the wonders
one can see out of the other eye.

An Ambulance Pulls up to The National Aquarium

We hope it's not because
an octopus had a heart attack.

We Arrive in Baltimore to Find The Entire City Under Construction

Pedestrian walkways, every corner,
the sides of building. There are noises

coming from underground. You can't
walk half a foot without an orange cone

accosting you. This is better then trash
lining the streets but one should focus

on the insides of buildings these days.
Another ambulance drives by. A citizen

must have gotten too close. We clutch
our forks and knives. We napkin on our lap.

The waffles are coming. The waffles are coming.
Every kind of berry you can imagine.

The American Dream

Miss Shirley's on Pratt Street
Offers an *Omelette to Call Your Own*
which is all I ever wanted out of America.

At the National Aquarium

I
We finish breakfast.
Head down the street
to see some
American fish.

II
The flounder fish are bigger than our heads
and they're not too shy about reminding us of that.

III
One exhibit in development
has completely motionless fish
as if they haven't been turned on yet.

IV
The fish that look like metal
seem to be in a hurry. Probably
long lines at the fish shinery.

V
I'm particularly fond
of the catfish here
because of mine at home
which are just cats.

VI
One fish has learned to swim backwards.
The other fish look to him like he is a fish God.

VII
The black ghost knife fish
is called upon to operate the
fish haunted houses and
whenever loaves of bread
are in need of slicing.

VIII
Three tanks next to each other are labeled
Climbing, Hiding and *Slurping*.
I head straight to *Slurping*.

IX
One aggressive fish
is kept separate from all
the other fish. Colloquially,
he is known as the *son of bitch fish*.

X
One fish looks exactly like a cone
and recently got side work on
a walkway.

XI
I want to ask Addie to moo at the cowfish
to lure it over for a picture. But some things
are better just imagined.

XII
I feel weird looking
at the blind fish.

XIII
Now I regret not
asking Addie to moo.

XIV
There is a third restroom at the aquarium
with just a picture of a fin on the door.
Don't go looking for it though as I will
deny this conversation ever happened.

XV
I think some of the pipes are crossed.
When I turned on the drinking fountain
a school of minnow came out.

XVI
At the cafe there is a sign suggesting
you can change the world one spoon at a time.
I'm going to go ahead and send an entire set of
cutlery to the middle east to see
if I can speed things along.

XVII
I misread a sign that says *fire extinguisher*
as *fish extinguisher* which is the gravest possible
mistake of literacy you could make here.

XVIII
We encounter two turtles making out.
Fortunately I always have a curtain with me
for such situations.

XIX
The terrible poison dart frog
got his name because of the disrespectful
manner in which he treated his mother.

XX
One family
in front of the frog habitats
agree the frogs all look fake.
This is the same group of people
who denied the moon landing
and the existence of Mister T
who I once saw in the wilds
of network television
clutching a pair of
Chinese stress balls.

XXI
Some fish move so quickly
they miss their opportunity
to be documented by my
brilliant fishisms.

XXII

One fish, barely motionless
hovers with its alligator mouth
wide open, waiting for food to swim in.
This is how I'm going to behave
at restaurants from now on.

XXIII

The level of excitement which
emanates from Addie when she discovers
a little fish following a similar big fish
cannot be measured on today's
scientific instruments.

XXIV

Every now and then
they drop a human arm
into the shark tank
to scare humanity
into submission.

XXV

The sawfish will come in handy
when the fish kingdom develops
an interest in going into construction.

XXVI

Addie is enjoying
the cute kids at the aquarium
as much as the fish.

We could have
gone to a playground and
saved seventy dollars

XXVII
One dolphin kind of looks like
he's talking to himself, like he's
a bitter old man who wishes things
were the way they used to be.

XXVIII
A sign in the bathroom says
A sperm whale bladder holds 44 times
more urine than "your" bladder does.

I suspect it's the NSA that has been
passing on information about my bladder
to the National Aquarium.

XXIX
Scallops have no brains
so they're very easy to
take advantage of.

XXX
Addie is excited
when I tell her that she is
my favorite mammal.

XXXI
The toothless catfish got its name
after a lifetime of poor dentistry.

XXXII
I'm not sure why the National Aquarium
gift shop is selling *Lolita* branded wine glasses.

XXXIII
I'm also not sure why the National Aquarium
is surrounded by seafood restaurants.

XXXIV
The weird part about the
*Paint Your Own Exotic Wildlife
Aquatic Play Set* is that
it comes with a set of paints
and live caucasian animals.

XXXV
Reality check:
They actually do serve seafood
in the aquarium cafe.

XXXVI
An orthodox family walks through the aquarium
pointing out to each other which fish they are allowed to eat.
I'm not sure if they're doing this as an educational piece,
to constantly remind themselves of the laws of Kashrut.
Or if they're concerned something's going to go down and
they might be trapped here for quite a while.

Need More Room

There aren't enough pages in this book to go into the ramifications of the restaurant here called *Dick's Last Resort.*

The Truth is Revealed

I make a loud, crazy yawning noise,
as I am want to do, while yawning
in the cafe and now a woman and her
two young children think I'm a crazy person.

Eastward Ho

You can pay money to paddle a dragon
out into the inner harbor. The fire breathing
apparatus has been disabled though.
I tell Addie we could paddle one of these
all the way to London. I receive no
acknowledgement from her camp on this.

On My Eventual Wet

The inevitability of falling into
the harbor is consuming me.

Contingency

I tell Addie the plan is
if we ever get separated
immediately destroy her cell phone
walk into the nearest subway
(restaurant or transport center)
pray to the first god that comes to mind
and then meet me at home in Los Angeles.
We'll have Jude shipped later.
She does not think any of this
is a good plan.

Sangriafest Destiny

I
A white wine grapefruit sangria
is the only civilized way to experience
5:00 in Baltimore. Thank you
hotel complimentary wine hour.
You take the museums right
out of my legs.

II
I continue to kiss Addie
long after she has left for the
other side of the room.
It may have been the sangria kissing.

Refuse

There should not be
a discarded Pepsi cup
in the fountain at the
Holocaust Memorial.

A Thing Addie Wants Included But Doesn't Want to Put Out Her Own Book.

All places called *Little Italy*
should be abbreviated as *Litaly*.

At Dinner, Steve Demanded a Poem

Congratulations Steve. You've made it!

Fire Alarm at the Hotel

Eight AM. We walk down
fourteen flights of stairs.
Each one a *Masada*.
Forget the desirability of
high floor.

Plans develop half way down.
We will walk right to Poe's grave.
We will walk right to breakfast
as if it was our plan all along.
Rain at the bottom reminds us

of the three umbrellas in our room,
fourteenth floor. We learn to hate
the smoking man at the bottom.
His smoke in everyone's nostril.
His ash a reminder of what might be.

How polite the voice of the alarm.
How convenient the visible rain.
Seize the day.

Haiku

for Brendan Constantine

Every time I
sneeze, I think about how much
you would enjoy it.

Dawn of the Lizard People

Addie is reflecting on our time with Audrey last night
She says *we are a lot alike. We both like eggplant parmigiana
And we are both lizard people.*

I'm sure she said some other things but I get stuck on
my wife as one of the *lizard people.* What do I really
know about her tongue?

Do I need to stock up on crickets, replace the house lights
with special UV rays? It doesn't matter, through sickness
and through health.

Through amphibious revelations,
'til death do us part.

Jon Told Us He Was Going Back in Time

After getting his doctorate and years in his field
he took a sabbatical and lived a year in a college dorm.
Soon he's heading back to his pre-school for some reason.
I warn him not to go back up inside his mother
and he turns redder than every tomato that ever was.

Disillusioned

We pass by the Baltimore Hippodrome
No one can tell me why there aren't
hippopotami inside.

(I'd rather the correct word be
Hippopotamusses.)

It Was a Dark and Stormy Morning

The only day we really experienced rain
was the morning we visited Poe's grave.

I'd like to tell you the sun burned away the clouds
moments after we paid our respects.

But, no, he made sure we experienced his weather
for hours after we left. Oh adopted son of Baltimore,

your life and death are in our memories
evermore.

Elevated Speech

The elevator voice which
announces the floors at our hotel
sounds like Eeyore, going down,
and a sexy temptress with all the
hope of a new day, going up.
I can't tell you how turned on
we get when she says *lobby*.

At the Baltimore Museum of Art

I
Much of the Baltimore Museum of Art is under renovation.
Consequently the only painting on display is a splotch of blue
a guy spilled on a piece of wood. We stare at it for hours
to get our money's worth at this free museum.

II
We see many portraits of little boys
in dresses as was the custom of the time.
These days little boys don't put on dresses
for many years and sometimes never
take them off.

III
Bust of Jean-Léon Gérome
Jean-Baptiste Carpeaux, 1827-1885

The bust of Jean Leon Gérome
looks like Edgar Allan Poe
Plus it's a disembodied head.

IV
The Thinker
August Rodin, 1902

We see an extra large *Thinker*.
To think of how many of his midget
brothers we've seen all over the world.

V
We enter the museum's *Cone Collection.*
Not a single cone is present.

VI
The Cone Sisters (no relation)
turned away from Picasso
during his cubist period.
He just put extra eyes on
everything so he could
see them anyway.

VII
A loud family surrounds me
in front of a dark forest by Klimt.
Their conversation reaching each other
in one of my ears and out the other.
We have invented the museum telegraph.
I head to the museum patent office.
Oh, there isn't one? Oh.

VIII
Still Life With Large Shell
Max Beckmann, 1939

This still life includes a living girl.
Perhaps she had herself petrified
for the painting.

IX
Still Life With Lemons
George's Braque, 1928

Still life with lemons
makes me think of
real life with iced tea.

X
Waterfall I
Georgia O'Keeffe, 1952

I learned from a TV show that Georgia O'Keefe's
paintings often looked like vaginas. I call this one
The Obscene Waterfall. Though I don't believe it.

XI
The changing of docents in the museum
is a ceremony to experience. A radio is passed
from one hand to another. Reserved smiles appear.
It is the only time they say anything besides
please take a step back.

XII
Headless Woman
Alberto Giacometti, 1932-1936 (1960 casting)

In honor of my four year old's obsession
I call this sculpture, *the tushy experience.*

XIII
Oxidation Painting
Andy Warhol, 1978

Visitors urinated
on a chemically treated canvas.

Later it hangs
in a museum.

Even later, poet brings
autograph pen into bathroom
for adoring fans.

XIV
The artist painted *Won't*.
But apparently he did
anyway.

XV
Interpretations of 'Chandelier with Hands'
Thomas Hirschhorn, 2006

Addie:
It's a handorah.

Rick:
This is what happens to you
When you die.

XVI
My latest thing is
whenever one of us leaves
to go to the bathroom
I will say *see you soon*.

XVII
One exhibit is called
Dialogue Between Painting and Sculpture.
But if you listen close enough it turns out
they're just talking about what they had for lunch.

XVIII
One ancient sculpture
is probably not called
Guy with Half his Head Missing.
But it could be.

XIX
Bags and Bottles

In the Gift Shop
after hyperventilating over a strawberry coin purse
Addie sees a canvas bag reusable bottle
combining two of her greatest loves.

we go home to
our east coast home
before going home

Rain

I
Were driving through a *classic nor'easter*.
He's going to feel it tomorrow.

II
The rain informs much of our trip from its perspective.
For example, the Chesapeake Bay refers to Baltimore
as *the occupation.* The water falls on our feet.
No two drops the same.

The Long Road Ahead

We spend five hours driving between
Baltimore and Allentown. It shouldn't
take that long but the rain and every car
that ever was joined us on the highway.
This is a communal day dream. We hope
they're not all heading to the same
gas station by the airport. We hope
the other place doesn't run out of sandwiches.
I've got my heart set on a caprese
hundreds of wet miles away.
My wife has never had to pee so bad.

Not Going to Happen

I message Brendan to tell him
They say its only an hour's drive to the moon
so we should meet there for lunch.

He writes back *yeah but I'm on foot.*
Forget about it, I tell him.
I'm not driving to Los Angeles to pick him up.

That would add three days to the trip.

Aberdeen

Driving northbound on ninety five
I take exit twenty two to Aberdeen
where I assume, Matthew, you have
been waiting for me this whole time

A Quickie

On the way to Philadelphia airport
we pass by what looks like a stone igloo.
I assume this is where the Flintstone Eskimos lived.

Still Life with Four Year Old on Tarmac

We spend days on the Chicago tarmac.
We think the pilot is trying to drive to Los Angeles.
This plane still has that *new plane smell.*
A woman from an old country walks the aisle
towards the bathroom. This is against all the laws.
But where she comes from, this is her way.
Another woman operates electronic devices
during the forbidden hour. A fire alarm in
the control tower has caused all these delays
and the civilians on our plane are considering
seceding from The Union. A four year old
sleeps between our seated legs. This will
make it awkward to watch the movie.
We may never see our luggage again.

Are You Still Reading?

The book is over now.
You should go home.

The author in his original career as a Union Soldier

About The Author

Two-time Pushcart Prize nominee Rick Lupert has been involved in the Los Angeles poetry community since 1990. He was awarded the Beyond Baroque Distinguished Service Award in 2014 for service to the Los Angeles poetry community. He served for two years as a co-director of the Valley Contemporary Poets, a non-profit organization which produces readings and publications out of the San Fernando Valley. His poetry has appeared in numerous magazines and literary journals, including *The Los Angeles Times, Rattle, Chiron Review, Red Fez, Zuzu's Petals, Stirring, The Bicycle Review, Caffeine Magazine, Blue Satellite* and others. He edited the anthologies *Ekphrastia Gone Wild - Poems Inspired by Art, A Poet's Haggadah: Passover through the Eyes of Poets*, and *The Night Goes on All Night - Noir Inspired Poetry*, and is the author of fifteen other books: *Nothing in New England is New, Death of a Mauve Bat, Sinzibuckwud!, We Put Things In Our Mouths, Paris: It's The Cheese, I Am My Own Orange County, Mowing Fargo, I'm a Jew. Are You?, Feeding Holy Cats, Stolen Mummies, I'd Like to Bake Your Goods, A Man With No Teeth Serves Us Breakfast* (Ain't Got No Press), *Lizard King of the Laundromat, Brendan Constantine is My Kind of Town* (Inevitable Press) and *Up Liberty's Skirt* (Cassowary Press). He has hosted the long running Cobalt Café reading series in Canoga Park since 1994 and is regularly featured at venues throughout Southern California.

Rick created and maintains the Poetry Super Highway, an online resource and publication for poets. (PoetrySuperHighway.com)

Currently Rick works as a music teacher at synagogues in Southern California and as a graphic and web designer for anyone who would like to help pay his mortgage.

Rick's Other Books

Ekphrastia Gone Wild (edited by)
Ain't Got No Press ~ July, 2013

Nothing in New England is New
Ain't Got No Press ~ March, 2013

Death of a Mauve Bat
Ain't Got No Press ~ January, 2012

The Night Goes On All Night
Noir Inspired Poetry (edited by)
Ain't Got No Press ~ November, 2011

Sinzibuckwud!
Ain't Got No Press ~ January, 2011

We Put Things In Our Mouths
Ain't Got No Press ~ January, 2010

A Poet's Haggadah (edited by)
Ain't Got No Press ~ April, 2008

A Man With No Teeth
Serves Us Breakfast
Ain't Got No Press ~ May, 2007

I'd Like to Bake Your Goods
Ain't Got No Press ~ January, 2006

Stolen Mummies
Ain't Got No Press ~ February, 2003

Brendan Constantine is My Kind of Town
Inevitable Press ~ September, 2001

Up Liberty's Skirt
Cassowary Press ~ March, 2001

Feeding Holy Cats
Cassowary Press ~ May, 2000

I'm a Jew, Are You?
Cassowary Press ~ May, 2000

Mowing Fargo
Sacred Beverage Press ~ December, 1998

Lizard King of the Laundromat
The Inevitable Press ~ February, 1998

I Am My Own Orange County
Ain't Got No Press ~ May, 1997

Paris: It's The Cheese
Ain't Got No Press ~ May, 1996

For more information:
http://PoetrySuperHighway.com/

Made in the USA
Coppell, TX
08 January 2023

10723738R00118